The 5-Figure Formula

The 5-Figure Formula

The Ultimate Guide to Reaching Your First 5-Figure Month

Kaila Uli

Published by Game Changer Publishing

Paperback ISBN: 978-1-963793-99-4
Hardcover ISBN: 978-1-964811-00-0
Digital: ISBN: 978-1-964811-01-7

www.GameChangerPublishing.com

Read This First

Just to say thank you for buying and reading my book, I would like to give you a few free bonus gifts, no strings attached!

To Download Your Free Gifts, Scan the QR Code:

The 5-Figure Formula

The Ultimate Guide to Reaching
Your First 5-Figure Month

Kaila Uli

www.GameChangerPublishing.com

Table of Contents

Introduction 1

Chapter 1 – Why the First Five Figures a Month Are So Critical 7

Chapter 2 – How to Create a Killer Value Proposition 11

Chapter 3 – Establishing Trust and Credibility 19

Chapter 4 – Setting Realistic Sales Goals 27

Chapter 5 – Mastering Brand Storytelling and Identity 31

Chapter 6 – Maximizing Your Website's Potential 37

Chapter 7 – Creating a Sales Funnel 41

Chapter 8 – Turning Social Media into an Active Sales Channel 47

Chapter 9 – Creating Compelling Content 51

Chapter 10 – Getting More Traffic to Your Website 59

Chapter 11 – Photography 63

Chapter 12 – Creating High-Conversion Listings 69

Chapter 13 – Pricing Products for Profit 73

Chapter 14 – Using Customer Service to Drive Sales 77

Chapter 15 – Building Your Email and SMS List 81

Chapter 16 – Identifying Key Marketing Channels 89

Chapter 17 – Analyzing and Optimizing Your Marketing Strategy 99

Conclusion and Next Steps 105

Introduction

My name is Kaila Uli, and this is the story of how I got started in business and why I'm doing what I'm doing. To give you some context about me, I am a mixed kid, Dutch and Indonesian. My grandparents immigrated from Indonesia to the Netherlands and eventually to the United States, starting a whole new life here. This translated to me growing up with not a lot. I grew up very, very poor. It was not the fun kind of poor, but the kind where you color your toes with black markers to make sure the other kids don't see the holes in your shoes. I hated that. We struggled, wondering where the next meal was coming from half the time and whether we would have electricity.

There were periods in my parents' life when we had a little bit more, but usually, we just didn't have anything. At a really young age, when I was about five, I had the epiphany that there are 8 billion people in the world and, if I could just figure out a way to get just one dollar from each of them, all of my problems would be solved. From that point on, I always tried to come up with a way to sell something. I tried selling rocks and getting those little catalogs where you go door to door and sell Tootsie Rolls to your neighbors to win a prize. I tried everything.

By the time I hit high school, I had taken an interest in business building and was learning as much as I could about it. To fast forward a bit, I went on to get married when I was 19. My husband and I dreamed of building a business together as soon as he got out of the Marines, but he got sick. He was diagnosed with cancer and given one year to live, but he passed away within four months. I was left with no money, a lot of bills, and a truck. Unfortunately, the truck was my husband's, and the government was not willing to give it to me, so I had to fight them to even get that.

I had nothing, so I thought to myself, *All right, I'll get a job. I'll try to make a life for myself.* It turns out no one will hire you if you don't have at least an associate's degree, which I did not. I decided then and there I was going to go to college. I didn't have money for it, but I thought that this was what I had to do to get a job. Now we hit the next roadblock: I had been homeschooled my entire life. Because of that, I didn't have a real diploma. I couldn't get into any colleges, even if I had the money. I had nowhere to go.

I realized that even if I got a job at McDonald's, I would not be able to cover my bills. Working all day, every day, 40 hours a week, I wouldn't even have enough money to keep 50 cents in my savings account at the end of the month. I decided to take a gamble on starting a business. This meant I had to have a job as well as a side hustle online.

After giving it some thought, I decided to make jewelry. I had $50 to start. That was it, $50 and nothing else, so I used the money to buy a little bit of inventory, things like cords, charms, and pendants. Then I started making necklaces by hand, and I sold them on Etsy. To my huge surprise, a small handful of people bought them. Within a day, I had sold my first necklace, and I continued to sell a necklace every few days. This little business gave me a couple of extra hundred dollars a month.

Ultimately, I stopped the jewelry business because it wasn't scalable. It took six hours of work to make one necklace worth $50. I realized after a few months that I just couldn't do that. So, I moved on to making soaps and candles. This business did a little better. I'd figured out how to market a bit better, and I was once again making a few hundred dollars a month. This business turned out to be unsustainable, too, because of the amount of labor that went into it, but the profit margins were higher, so I had a little bit more money now to start my third business.

My third business was craft packaging supplies. There was this very special bottle that crafters wanted, but you had to buy them in huge packs of 100, and nobody had the funds for that. I bought the big pack, broke it apart into units of two or three, and then resold them to crafters for $20 or $30. Crafters wanted this bottle badly, and my plan worked really well. I did this for about a year, but eventually, the business became my third failure. Like my first two businesses, this one wasn't scalable, either. In this case, the market just wasn't big enough. Even though sales were what I considered good, they would never reach $10,000, $20,000 a month, because there just weren't enough people who wanted what I was selling. Additionally, moving into the big crafter space, like mass-market crafters, would have required a lot of capital, which I didn't have.

I started again with Brillies Sunglasses, and the business became my first big success. This time, I went in with all the knowledge I had learned from my failed businesses. By now, I had earned enough money to have gone to college. I had a marketing degree and a business degree, all the education that had come with them, and extra money. I started this business with inventory and a website and did it the right way. I knew I had struck gold because my first sale happened within 30 minutes of going live.

At that point, I went crazy with it. I wasn't rich by any means. I just had a little more money. I started making deals with suppliers for consignment, like, "I'll give you 50% upfront and then 50% when we sell it." I traded my time with people who had access to a vintage sunglasses inventory. I did marketing for them in exchange for product discounts. I worked with whomever I could get in touch with just to be on their set or in their presence to meet celebrities and people who could propel my business forward, and it worked. We partnered with a guy called "The Schmo," podcaster Dave Schmulenson, one of the UFC's biggest personalities, and made him custom glasses.

The glasses have been on all of the *Sports Illustrated* models since 2019. We have worked with Amazon, Hulu, and magazines *Harper's Bazaar, Glamour, Vogue*—all of the big ones. There's a documentary called *The Curse of Von Dutch: A Brand to Die For*, which is very popular on Hulu, and we supplied them with vintage items for that. That is how I got to where I am, building off of failures until I hit a success.

I wrote this book because I came from poverty. I didn't know how to speak the language of business, and I didn't have the resources or even know where to go or what to do to start one. Anyone can google how to start a business, but the information you get is basic and not very helpful. I want to bridge that gap for people trying to do exactly that, explaining the process in terms anyone can understand. I want to make what I learned over the last 10 years available to everybody.

This program is called the 5-Figure Academy because that's the foundation of your business. You hear a lot about getting your business to six figures a month, but you won't get there without consistently hitting five figures a month first—and not just once because you went viral, but consistently, several months in a row. Only then can you start to think about bigger things. This book exists to get you to your first five figures, and you can expect to learn exactly how to do that. All you need to do is follow the recipes I've done myself time and time again, the strategies I use in all my businesses, broken down into bite-sized pieces of information.

CHAPTER 1

Why the First Five Figures a Month Are So Critical to Your Success

Generating $10,000 in monthly revenue is a huge milestone for small businesses because it proves viability. It shows you have something that enough people are interested in to support growth in that market. It indicates there are interested audiences. If you're having a hard time hitting five figures a month, often it can be attributed to not enough people wanting what you're selling. This is a common trap for small business owners. We love something so much that we think everyone else must love it, too. But then we struggle for sales because not a lot of people love it like we do.

Hitting five figures consistently, month over month, shows good viability and interest. It also demonstrates you have a good understanding of your target audience, their pain points, what they're looking for, and how to communicate with them. This means you can scale up. You just find more customers. It shows you have a really good understanding of your marketing channels. This is a big deal because your customers exist on specific channels, whether they're Snapchat and Facebook users, TikTok and YouTube watchers, or Google searchers. It shows you know where they're spending time, and you have figured out not only that but also how to communicate with them in their time on their chosen platforms. Essentially, it proves future growth.

Here's a story about my own experience with this. When I sold jewelry and soap, even though I was making a sale a day, sometimes three sales a day, there wasn't enough customer interest to support growth. Now, jewelry and soaps are pretty mass market, so you would think there would be billions of potential customers. However, the problem with the jewelry was that I sold unique items to people with very specific tastes. There just weren't enough people out there who wanted those specific things. With the soap, I sold coffee-infused bars, supposedly good for your skin, but they were very heavy, dense, and greasy. The only people who bought them had a specific interest in nature, organics, and coffee scents but were fine with greasy soaps. Not a lot of people want a greasy soap. Sure, people bought my soap every day, but it still wasn't enough to be a big business.

Compare those two business ventures to the early days of Brillies, the vintage sunglasses business. With Brillies, the first sale happened within 30 minutes, and the sales never really stopped. That's the difference between having something people truly desire versus something you're trying to push them to desire.

Now, I want you to think about what five figures a month means for you. What would making that kind of revenue mean for your life and the current position of your business? How would that change what you're doing? Would it change how you feel about yourself? Would it change the opportunities your business can take? Almost assuredly, the answer to all these questions is yes because, when you hit that five figures a month, it gives you a lot more flexibility to grow. It gives you the potential to hire, run ads, and start paying for PR placements. It even gives you more flexibility to start sending a greater volume of influencer packages. Hitting five figures a month is a clear indicator that your business is on the right track. It means you have something people want, and you're able to generate significant revenue from it. It also shows you have a bigger shot at opportunities like expansion or scaling.

To get five figures a month, you need a solid understanding of your target audience and what they need, and you have to effectively market to them. It's as simple as creating compelling offers, optimizing your website and landing pages, and leveraging social media. But the most important thing you need to hit five figures a month is a growth mindset. Being willing to learn, change things when you need to, and take criticism is crucial.

You're here because you're not a business pro. You probably didn't start on the right foot, and that's fine because we've all been there. But you have to be able to find your blind spots and correct them. You can't be stubborn; you have to be impartial, put emotions aside, learn where you went wrong, and right the ship. Learn where to take risks and where to dial in.

CHAPTER 2

How to Create a Killer Value Proposition

Let's talk about why value propositions are important. An effective value proposition is a clear, concise statement that communicates the unique value of your product or service. Many people miss this or don't understand just how critical it is to closing a sale. Essentially, in a handful of words, the value proposition tells the shopper exactly what you're about, why you're different from competitors, and why they should choose you. That's it.

Your value proposition will have a massive impact on sales because it's one of the first things customers see when they land on your website. A strong value proposition will get someone's attention within just a few seconds and compel them to take action. A weak value proposition, one that is unclear, risks leaving them confused. This leads to them being disengaged, which leads to "I'm not going to buy this from you."

A great example of an effective value proposition is the Dollar Shave Club's "Shave Time. Shave Money." In just a few short words, you know what they sell, the price point, and that it will save you time. The value proposition is short, sweet, and simple, yet it encompasses the entire brand. When crafting your value proposition, you want to dial in on what makes your product so great. To help you do this, I'm going to break the process down into a few chunks.

First, before you even think about starting, you need to figure out a few things: your product name, target audience, customers' challenges, product features, and user benefits. All of these will come in handy as you craft your brand value proposition.

The next step is to identify your target audience and understand their needs and pain points. Once you have that information, you can craft a message that actually speaks to them. It's important that you address their specific challenges. This is not the place to be vague. This is where you prove, "I know you, and I know this is what you want." The more you know your target audience, the better your value proposition is going to be.

After that, highlight the unique benefit your product offers that competitors don't. That's key. We can all think about something that makes us "better," but what makes us better than our competitors? This can be anything, like faster delivery times, personalization, and great customer service. But it has to be something your competitors can't do. Really highlight this. Make it clear so your audience can immediately understand what it is that sets you apart and that they can't get with anyone else. VRBO's value proposition provides an

excellent example of this: "Where Families Travel Better Together."
The "better" drives home the point that competitors can't provide
the same quality of service.

Next, you're going to test your value proposition because
sometimes we think we have done something great, but then it turns
out to be not so great. The example I like to use for this is when
you're a kid and you're playing the piano. You think you sound like
Beethoven, and the music is the most beautiful thing ever, but to
everyone else in the room, it's painful noise. We don't always get it
right the first time. It's really important to test your value
proposition, but the testing doesn't have to be massive. You can get
feedback from friends, customers, whoever, and make adjustments.
Remember, your value proposition is not one-and-done. It's a living
document. It evolves with your business and your audience's needs.
Just because you have a killer one this year, it may not be the one
you use next year. That's completely fine.

Now, let's dig into the meat and potatoes of what makes a good
value proposition. They take a lot of time. Keep in mind that this is
a summary of your entire brand condensed into just a few small
words, at most, a powerful paragraph. Don't worry about bum-
rushing it and trying to get it done in an hour because that's not
going to happen. A strong value proposition needs to have a hook,
meaning it quickly and clearly communicates "why" and "what."
This hook needs to speak to your audience and communicate your
brand's promise to them, so keep it relevant to your target.

The one thing a lot of people miss when crafting a value proposition is that it needs to show quantifiable value. What I mean by this is that the value can't be some vague thing like "hand-poured with love" or "custom candles that make your home smell great." These are not value propositions because there's no quantifiable value there. Quantifiable value is like "Shave Time. Shave Money." It tells me exactly what real, tangible value I'm immediately getting out of the product. Avoid any filler, fluffy words like "artisanal" and "handcrafted with love." If it doesn't offer real, tangible value, do not put it in your value proposition. The value proposition is going to be the first thing your visitors see when they go to your website, homepage, landers, and even social media bio, so it needs to show real value as effectively and quickly as possible.

Here's an exercise to help you narrow down your value proposition. Explain to your friend, without using any buzzwords or jargon, what you sell, what you do, and what the benefits are. Focus on the specific things that make your business better than your competitors. No ambiguity. Just tell them.

Give them the elevator pitch of what you sell, and see if they get it. If they do, great, you're going to take what you said and boil it down to a more impactful paragraph. From that paragraph, refine it even further to a few words. This is going to take some time. It'll probably take you a few drafts before you have your perfect value proposition, but that's normal.

Now we're going to talk about clarifying your brand's mission and purpose. This will help you get a clear vision of your value proposition. If you're having a hard time communicating your brand messaging, you probably don't have a strong enough purpose. That is going to keep you at arm's length from your shoppers because they'll feel it. Shoppers are smart. They know if you're being transparent and honest with them about what your core values are. You need to be able to identify who you are and why you're in business. If you can communicate that to your customers in a meaningful way, you are already light years ahead of the competition. Your purpose is the reason your brand exists. Who is it for? Your vision is the future you are looking towards. What are you helping to create in this world? And your values are the principles that drive you. What do you believe in? Not always, but some people incorporate politics into their selling points.

Next, we're going to dig into your competitive edge. Your value proposition needs to draw people to you like a magnet. And who are you pulling them away from? The competition. To do this, you have to know your advantages and tell them to the customer. I know, I keep saying it over and over, "Communicate it to the customer," but a lot of people miss that. It's one thing to know what your values and advantages are, but are you spelling them out for the customer? That's the make-or-break point. What makes my product stand out? Is my shipping faster? Is my copy smarter? Is it sexier? Am I the only one doing it? Does my straightening iron straighten your hair better and faster than the other guys' irons or give it a silkier, smoother appearance?

Your competitive edge can really be as simple as "My customer service is a thousand times better than anyone else's." That can actually be part of your value proposition. Now ask yourself, *What do I have that could be proprietary? No one else has it. It's my trade secret, and you can only get it from me.* You might also ask, *Am I the cheapest?* or *Am I the most luxurious?* These are all points you can use to actually separate yourself from the competition and pull customers towards you.

Next, you need to use the proper tone. Your value proposition is not written for you. It's written for the people you want to reach. It needs to connect with them, not just mentally but emotionally. This is where knowing your audience comes into play. You need to gather as much insight as possible about them to understand how to talk to them in the right tone. You want to know who they are, what they care about, how they like to be communicated with, what words they respond well to, and what words they think are corny and cringe. The more you understand these things, the easier it'll be to write a proposition that makes them happy and excited and gets their attention.

Once you have all this data in front of you, it's time to make a big list of all the benefits you can think of for your product or service. Then, you're going to write a draft of your value statement. This is probably the hardest part of creating one and will probably take you the most time. It is where you start actually putting together the best, most exciting, most relevant, most unique points about your business. It's worth spending a lot of time on. If your list ends with 50 points, that's great. We want it all so we can extract the juiciest, most exciting bits to make your value proposition crush.

After all that's done, you test. You've crafted this tight little paragraph of benefits, and it's going to go somewhere on your homepage where it will be easily visible. You can try out a few positions. I recommend you place your value proposition directly below your "hero image"—that's the big, beautiful image right at the top of your website. Once you've got it in place, it's time to see if it leads to higher conversions. If you've done it right, once it's implemented, you should start seeing more conversions.

Let's look at a few more examples of effective value propositions. Slack's is "Where work happens." Even if you don't know what Slack is, if you're in the early stages of looking for a communication platform and you see this slogan, it just makes sense. You know Slack is a productive space where you're going to get a lot done, and it's going to be easy to use. People on the back end of Slack are just making it happen, making a million bucks. In just three simple words, Slack's value proposition communicates the company's mission to improve communication and collaboration.

Another effective value proposition is Airbnb's "Belong anywhere." Two words. They know their target audience has a desire for unique, authentic travel experiences rather than just going to a regular old hotel. With just two words, they communicate their promise to provide a home away from home anywhere in the world. Magical. Amazing. Belong anywhere.

Now it's time to create your own killer value proposition. And don't feel rushed. It takes time. Give yourself that grace. Understand that the more time you take to craft one, the better it's going to be. That is how you make a value proposition that resonates with your target audience and drives sales.

CHAPTER 3

Establishing Trust and Credibility

Trust is critical to converting a casual browser into a buyer. When customers trust a business or brand, they're way more likely to buy from them, make repeat purchases, and recommend the business to others. On the other hand, when customers don't trust a business, they're probably going to abandon the site, feel negatively toward the brand, and might even share negative feedback in comment sections or with friends and family.

How do you establish trust and credibility with your audience? First and foremost, be transparent and honest. This sounds kinda cliché, but remember, things that don't seem "tricky" to you can be seen as deceptive by the customer. For example, if you say you provide "free shipping," but in tiny little letters, it says "with a purchase over $120," that can feel like a trick. Not only is the required purchase amount high, especially if you're selling low-cost goods, but you also tried to "hide" it. You've got to think like a shopper.

A real-world example of this is a cleaning service I hired. They charged $45 an hour and offered a new-user discount of 50% off initial services. However, in teeny, tiny, almost invisible text, they indicated that by accepting the offer, I was looped into a year-long contract at $250 a month. Now, technically, I was in the wrong… because, technically, this was disclosed, but I felt scammed and deceived, and now I go out of my way to warn people about them. You don't want to be that brand.

You also need to provide excellent customer service. Respond quickly to inquiries and issues and go above and beyond to ensure that customers are satisfied with their experience.

Let's talk about one of the most powerful ways to build trust: social proof. This means leveraging customer reviews, testimonials, and case studies that show the value of your product or service on your site, your social media, and wherever your brand "lives." When you're small, share every post that people have tagged you in. Leave comments on other people's pages to start building a presence online. Consider sending gifts and products to smaller creators, who are usually happy to create posts around your products for free or low cost in exchange for a post you can repost to your own page. Start building momentum. Respond to every reasonable comment you can.

Finally, it's important to be consistent in your messaging and branding. This means making sure all your marketing, website copy, photos, and social media content are aligned and share the same clear and consistent message about your business and products.

Here are a few examples of how e-commerce and service-based businesses can earn the trust of their shoppers:

E-commerce businesses:

1. Provide clear and detailed product descriptions. Such descriptions, including high-quality photos and videos, show that you're transparent about what you're selling. They prove to shoppers that you're a "real" business and help them feel more confident in their purchasing decisions.

2. Report good customer reviews and ratings. Having customer reviews and ratings on your product pages can build trust because it shows that other people vouch for the product. Keep in mind that having populated reviews is great for trust-building, but having no reviews can actually hurt conversion rates. So, do your best to get those filled out, but if you can't, it's better not to have them.

Service-based businesses:

1. Prominently display testimonials and case studies on your website. They show you have a proven track record of delivering results and give customers peace of mind that you can deliver on your promises.

2. Offer a bulletproof guarantee. Such a guarantee can erase customer concerns about being scammed or left with a subpar product or service. It shows that you stand behind your services and are committed to delivering results that meet their expectations. And make it big. If your offer doesn't scare you just a little, it's not bold enough to tempt the customer.

The flip side of increasing customer trust is mitigating perceived risk, which significantly impacts how shoppers make decisions about who to buy from. At its core, perceived risk includes all the little doubts customers have when choosing who to purchase from, and not mitigating it leads to no or low sales.

Perceived risk creates hesitation and second-guessing, leading to a decline in purchase intent. Shoppers delay or completely abandon their decision to buy when they perceive a high level of risk. For example, When shoppers aren't quite sure about the quality, functionality, or specifications of a product, they pause and second-guess the decision. Poorly written descriptions without tangible details, limited product images, or ambiguous information about features and benefits increase perceived risk.

Imagine that you're considering buying a phone online. If the product description is vague or doesn't have important details about the phone's specifications, camera quality, or battery life, you'll feel cagey about the product and seller. This ambiguity increases perceived risk because shoppers can't make an informed decision based on the available information.

Here are some steps you can take to mitigate perceived risk:

- Provide detailed product descriptions that highlight quality, features, and benefits.

- Post clear sizing charts, specifications, and measurements for clothing, shoes or other size-dependent items.

- Showcase customer reviews and testimonials to demonstrate social proof and reassure shoppers.

- Offer a hassle-free return policy to reduce shoppers' concerns about making the wrong choice. Remember, it's their money on the line.

- Implement a secure and user-friendly checkout process that protects customer information.

- Ensure your website is professional and user-friendly. This alone can greatly increase the confidence a shopper has in your brand.

- Maintain consistent brand messaging across all channels. This shows a shopper that you "really are" who you claim to be.

- Use high-quality product images that accurately represent the item and provide multiple angles or views. This is crucial. The shopper needs to feel, smell, touch, taste, and experience the product through your photos.

- Offer secure payment options, such as SSL encryption and trusted payment gateways.

- Provide responsive customer support to address inquiries and concerns quickly.

Next is enhancing the customer trust you're building. Here are some ways you can use communication and transparency to improve your relationship with customers:

- Make sure that product pricing, shipping fees, and any additional charges are clearly stated. Shoppers hate being surprised with extra fees when checking out.

- Display contact information clearly. Make it super easy for shoppers to reach you.

- Communicate shipping times and delivery estimates upfront, setting realistic expectations. For example, let's say you're a dropshipper with 10-day shipping. It's far better to overstate your delivery times and overperform than understate and leave shoppers frustrated and wondering where their packages are. This will break customer trust beyond repair.

- Maintain open lines of communication with customers, providing order confirmations, shipping notifications, and order tracking details.

- Be transparent about any product limitations, such as availability or variations in color or size.

These actionable steps can effectively manage perceived risk and create a more comfortable and trustworthy shopping experience for customers.

CHAPTER 4

Setting Realistic Sales Goals

Why do we need to have realistic sales goals? This isn't just a corny little thing people say. Having realistic sales goals is critical for keeping you motivated and your business chugging along because they give you something you can quickly work towards, and they keep you energized and motivated when you hit them. Numerous studies have shown that the reward center in the brain is activated when milestones are achieved.

There's a big difference between saying, "I want to hit $1,000 in sales in the next two weeks," versus, "I want to hit $60,000 in sales by the end of the year." One is very achievable and gives you something you can work hard towards in a short burst. When you hit that milestone, you're going to feel so good about yourself that you're going to have the energy to go on to the next: "Okay, I got my $1,000 in sales for these two weeks. For the next two weeks, I want to get $1,500." It gives you something to shoot for that you can attain quickly, and the reward of achieving it keeps you going.

On the other hand, when you create sales goals that are way too big, and there's no chance of you reaching them anytime soon, you are much less likely to have the motivation to keep going. The small goal gives us a reward hit two weeks from now, while the overly ambitious goal, even if we do everything right 100% of the time, may give us a reward by the end of the year, and even then, there's no guarantee.

Setting short, realistic, easily attainable sales goals also helps you maintain focus and keeps you on the right track. It gives you clear intentions on what you're trying to do right now. It gives you a sense of purpose, and it keeps you motivated to make consistent progress. Again, this may not feel like a big deal until you're actually doing it. Celebrating regular wins keeps your confidence high and gives you momentum. The data shows us that achieving smaller objectives adds fuel to the fire, keeps your passion going, and helps you tackle more significant goals.

This is all positive reinforcement that gives you a growth mindset. If you're anything like me, and I imagine a lot of small business owners are, it doesn't feel like you should be celebrating after $1,000 in sales. You want a million. You want ten million. But allowing yourself to celebrate these little milestones is going to give you the juice you need to carry through to the big ones.

Making small, realistic goals also helps you manage expectations and reduce unnecessary stress. Many small business owners, myself included, are guilty of setting the bar so high that they frequently feel frustrated, disappointed, and sad. Those negative feelings can send you on an emotional roller coaster ride, where you're tying your emotions to your sales and conversion rates for the month. That's not something you want to do. You'll find that you're in a much better mental state when you have these short little hits to keep you going.

Here's a real-life example of how this happened with my vintage sunglasses business. After my initial success, I was riding high and set an over-the-top expectation for myself. I overstocked on inventory, taking on tens of thousands of dollars more than I could actually handle. I thought, *If I buy the inventory, it's going to keep me motivated to the point where I hit multiple millions of dollars in sales by the end of this year.* What actually ended up happening was that I became overwhelmed by the purchase, and when I didn't see the kind of upward momentum I'd expected, I got more stressed out.

It's really important to make sure you manage your expectations and keep your stress low when it comes to sales goals. This is something I like to call "right-sizing," a term I learned from a mentor who worked as a security contractor for Apple. In his words, you should "right-size" everything in your business, including your expectations. Think about how you own and operate your business. We right-size our pricing, the size of our warehouses, and our purchases, correct? Right-size your expectations as well; it'll help you realistically adjust your sales goals.

Now, I know you're thinking, *I don't need to do that.* You're thinking that having the right expectations and a realistic sales goal is not for you. That's for the other guys. You're different because you're a boss-level entrepreneur. Nobody's going to slow you down. I really need you to understand that this will help you be that boss-level entrepreneur you are trying to be. I had to learn this the hard way. Don't do that. Setting realistic goals is a very simple step you can take to keep your momentum as an entrepreneur.

CHAPTER 5

Mastering Brand Storytelling and Identity for Five-Figure Sales

It's not enough these days to just sell a product. Those days are long gone. Customers' mindsets have flipped. They want to connect with brands that have the same values as them, and they want to understand the story behind the brand. Brand storytelling has existed throughout the history of marketing and sales, but it's happening now in a way that we haven't seen before. Shoppers are willing to spend more, wait longer on shipping times, and go above and beyond for brands they feel a connection with.

One great example of brand storytelling is Patagonia's "Don't Buy This Jacket" campaign. Patagonia is a multi-billion-dollar company with a large base of customers who trust them. They built that trust through campaigns such as this one, which was a big push to stop overconsumption. If you don't need something, don't buy it. If you need it, buy it. Simple yet extremely effective. The result was that millions of people bought the jacket because they resonated with the messaging: "I'm buying too much, so instead, I'm going to start buying from this brand Patagonia, which cares about the planet and sustainability." They're predicted to have their best sales year ever in 2024 because they've built such a strong connection with their customers.

People are tired of being advertised to, and they're tired of being told to buy things. They're tired of seeing their favorite influencers bought out by corporations and constantly telling them to buy this new that or the other thing. They want connection, which gives every small business a fighting chance to survive.

A big part of your brand storytelling is connecting with your shoppers. That's really what it is. Essentially, what you're doing is making sure the shopper understands your key identity, values, and purpose, and you do this through narratives. The difference between a good brand story and a lackluster or uninteresting one is sales.

First, your brand storytelling needs to be quick. When a shopper encounters your brand for the first time, you have less than three seconds to seal the deal with them. They make super-split decisions about whether or not they want to engage with you or go to the next guy, so your brand storytelling, wherever you're putting it, must be short, sweet, and to the point, and it's critical that the shopper gets it. Less than three seconds, that's what we're after.

The key elements of brand storytelling are pretty simple. You need a hero—the main person your brand portrays. Every brand's hero is a stand-in for the customer—the same pain points, lifestyle, and experiences.

Next, you need a conflict: what problem is the hero facing? This isn't some big, over-the-top thing. If I'm the hero in your brand story and I have really curly hair, but I want it to be straight, then I want a hair straightener. That is the conflict. I need straight, silky hair. That's the conflict your brand is going to offer the solution to in your storytelling. Don't overcomplicate it. A lot of people get stuck on this and think, *There's no hero in my brand,* or *There's no conflict in my brand.* There are. Without a hero and a conflict, you don't have brand storytelling. You just need to figure out who and what they are. Ultimately, your brand storytelling is going to provide a resolution for your hero. You're going to make a brand story that focuses on your unique selling proposition.

We talked about this a little bit earlier. Your unique selling proposition is what makes your product so special. With this in hand, you're going to make a relatable hero. As you do, think about all the target audience information you've gathered for your brand and how it might relate to this hero that you're creating. Once you have a hero, you need to establish the conflict. In plain words, this is where you identify the problems and challenges the hero faces. Then, you need to introduce a solution. The product is the solution. Plain and simple. Your product is the solution to the conflict for the hero, and you're going to introduce your product to the world as exactly that, demonstrating how your brand is so unique and special that it can solve the problem seamlessly.

Let's use Apple as an example. The hero in Apple's story is you. It's me. It's the customer. Apple makes us the hero because it knows this will be an emotional trigger for us, which is what we should all be trying to do. Apple's hero is creative, innovative, and not afraid to challenge the status quo. The funny thing is a lot of us aren't really like that, but we like to think that we are, and Apple has found a way to make us all feel like that as we buy their products. Buying an Apple product doesn't mean you're just buying, say, a phone. It means you're at the edge of technology. I'm an artist. I make music. I deeply enjoy the arts. Participating in Apple's story makes you this cool hero who is not afraid to go against the grain, even though you're buying the most-purchased products in the world.

The conflict for Apple is that other devices have limitations. They're not user-friendly. They're not super advanced. They're just normal. They're regular. By buying an Apple product, you're not part of the crowd. You're an innovator. You're creative. You're a free spirit. It really speaks to our need to be different.

The solution to the conflict, of course, is Apple products. Whether you're buying a Mac, an iPhone, or an iPad, it doesn't really matter. The Apple story tells you that they have the tools you need to overcome your limitations as an artist and break free from the system that's holding you back. You're getting access to this beautifully designed, powerful device that enables creativity and makes you an individual.

Just like Apple, you can use your brand storytelling to separate yourself from competitors in the marketplace. We live in a world where everyone has access to everything they need in real time. I know exactly where I can get a mug, hot sauce, a chair, anything I need, and I know how much it's going to cost. The only way you're going to pull me away from a brand is by offering me better storytelling and showing me how your brand is a better fit for me. You can do this by understanding what makes a hero feel special.

If I'm a shopper, and I'm well off, work at home, spend $5 a day on lattes, want to look like I'm rich, and am looking for leather chairs, what are you going to do to pull me to your business? What you're going to do is sell your leather chairs in a way that's better than the other guy. Sell it to me in a way that makes me feel like this is the chair that I can post on Instagram, and people are going to immediately know that I live an elevated lifestyle. That is how you do it. You use brand storytelling to pull people to you and make them feel like you have something special for them.

CHAPTER 6

Maximizing Your Website's Potential

Maximizing your website is a really big deal for small businesses because many of us build our own sites. This is fine, but it usually means that, unless you are a website professional, your website is likely not working as it should, and there's a good chance people can tell it was self-built, which is a conversion rate killer. Your website should be indistinguishable from those built by big professional brands. Shoppers shouldn't be able to say, "They definitely did this themselves." The reason is simple: customer expectations have skyrocketed due to ease of accessibility and the massive shift to online business. Shoppers' expectations for your website are very high. It's either professional or it's trash.

You don't want a website that makes shoppers think, *Oh, he must be running his business out of his garage.* There's nothing wrong with running a business from a garage or home; you just don't want it to appear that way. An amateurish site signals to shoppers that the business may not be trustworthy. It raises doubts about product contamination with dog hair, smoke, or handling by kids. Maybe the product was unboxed on TikTok and repackaged. A poorly built site leads to harsh judgments and likely no purchases.

Another big myth among small business owners is that consistency isn't that big of a deal. It is. Your branding photos, fonts, and colors need to be consistent across all your pages. This means using a commercial font that is professional, easy to read, and complements your brand. It needs to be "in-theme." It would be weird if you used Lobster font on a very serious site selling medical devices. However, you don't want the same font everywhere. Your site shouldn't read like a Word document. The font in your logo should be different from the rest of your site, and your title font should complement your description font. These fonts must be paired well and look great together. Think complementary, professional, and easy to read when choosing your fonts.

Next is your "hero image," a crucial yet often mishandled part of your site that can significantly boost sales. This tight shot of your product in use is one of the first things people see on your site. You have less than a second to capture shoppers' attention, so your hero image must be clear, crisp and vibrant. Stage your hero image to make it dynamic and directly showcase what's for sale.

Here's where it gets tricky. You want your image to be stylish while also making it clear what's for sale. The image needs to "sell the dream" without distracting from the core product. For example, if you sell blankets, it would be the kiss of death to drape one over a couch in a big room with 50 different pieces of decoration and no clear sight of what's actually for sale. Keep it tight. If you're struggling here, visit big players in your niche to understand how they use their hero images effectively.

Your CTA, or call to action, is generally a button or link that directs a shopper to their next step. They tell a shopper quickly and clearly what they should do next. CTAs need to be visible immediately upon landing on your site without scrolling. It must be short and simple, like "Shop Now."

While having an effective home page is crucial, that doesn't mean you can neglect the rest of your site. Your About page is also essential. Though not necessary for everyone, many shoppers will be interested in your background. Your website's header and footer are vital, too. The header should focus on shopping links, while the footer should contain factual information like return policies. Additionally, you need a contact page, which should be easily accessible from your footer. This page provides contact information to reassure potential customers.

Another often overlooked conversion killer is bad photos. These are your "window shops" and should be designed to suck shoppers in. High-quality photos are key. You need five to 10 photos per product, showing various angles and settings. Since shoppers can't handle the product in real life, these photos replace the in-store experience and give them the ability to smell, see, touch, and "experience" the product online.

Slow load times, confusing design, and poor mobile response are other conversion rate killers. Eighty-six percent of shoppers use mobile, meaning your site needs to load quickly and be easy to navigate. Banners should not tell your entire brand story. They are for one-sentence updates about current business news. Pop-ups, when used incorrectly, can be intrusive and annoying. Use them sparingly and ensure they integrate well with your brand.

Lastly, let me share a personal story from my Brillies business. I built my first website and was proud of it, but it was so poorly done that an ad agency refused to work with me. They insisted I get everything re-shot, create a real logo, improve icon placements, learn to make a proper CTA, and rebuild the entire site before considering my brand. This experience highlights the significance of having a well-designed site.

CHAPTER 7

Creating a Sales Funnel

If you've searched anywhere online or looked up how to build a business from scratch, you've heard of "funnels." They're sometimes presented as big and scary, but they're actually pretty simple. We're going to go over how to construct one in a really easy way. One of the best ways to think about a funnel is to imagine an upside-down triangle. The flat top of the triangle is the mouth of your funnel, where you bring your customers in.

The funnel has layers, and the idea is to move people down through these layers until they get to the point at the bottom, the conversion point. This is where people turn into a sale. At the top of the funnel, shoppers are the least warm to us and our product. They're just casual browsers looking at your product and a thousand others. They're not even aware that they want to buy what you're selling; they're just casually seeing it.

Imagine you're driving through LA and see a billboard promoting a new product. It's one you weren't aware existed, much less something you wanted; it's just a "thing." You're entering the awareness stage of that brand's funnel. Next, you might be exposed to some online ads or influencers wearing the product. As you get more exposure, if you're interested in the product, you'll warm up and move down the company's funnel. If they've done their marketing correctly, they'll eventually move you to the bottom of the funnel, where you'll say, "Hey, I actually like this. I want this. Where do I get it?" Now, you'll start comparing sites and outlets that sell this item. You'll shop around, looking for who has the best option. Maybe it's the initial company versus two others. Whichever you go with, they'll keep pulling you down their funnel until they get you to convert.

Funneling customers is a pretty simple process. The first thing we're going to do is define our target audience. Like everything else in business, nothing happens unless we know who we're talking to. We're going to define our target audience and start making content around them, directing ads at them, and ensuring our website speaks to them. We're going to start putting out feelers to attract these people into the top part of our funnel, the awareness stage. We're not going to get any sales here; we're just going to get people to understand that we exist.

Next comes the middle of the funnel, the interest or consideration stage. Now that they're aware our product exists, we're going to get them to intentionally search for us. We're providing valuable, relevant content tailored to them. The goal of this stage is to get people to see us as someone who knows what we're talking about. This is still not going to bring in sales, but it's going to start warming people up to us.

In the third part of our funnel, we're going to get them to start seeing us as more serious. This is where we start building relationships and trust with them. Maybe they'll turn into followers here. Maybe this is where they start commenting on our posts. They may not be ready to buy yet, but they will start seeing us as a value point as we interact with them.

Next, we nurture them, meaning we convince them to see our product as a potential future purchase. That doesn't mean they're going to buy from us, but they have warmed up to the product and now view it as something they can use in their life. We nurture them through things like email marketing, retargeting ads, and case studies.

- **Email marketing** targets interested email subscribers with updates and promotions about your products and brand.

- **Retargeting ads** follow people around online who've already visited your site or interacted with your brand, nudging them to come back and make a purchase.

- **Case studies** are like success stories that show off how you've helped clients or completed projects, which can help attract new customers by proving trustworthiness and credibility.

When customers visit our website, it means they have developed a real interest in our product. Once they're there, we expose them to testimonials or demos to show them how the product solves their problems.

Now that we've gotten them all warmed up, we try to convert them into a sale. This is the point at the bottom of our funnel where we hope somebody will choose us over the other guys. This is the action stage. We've got them in the mindset where they're ready to buy, and they want to buy from us. Now, we take our best shot at converting them into a sale with our fully built-out beautiful website. We've nurtured them for some time, and we have a great CTA that pushes them to purchase.

The final step of the funnel happens outside of the funnel triangle: retaining customers. Our funnel doesn't end with the purchase. We want to constantly bring people back. The great thing about bringing people back is they've already been warmed up, so converting them should be easier. If we're on point with our customer service and delivery of our product, we can now reach out to our repeat buyers and bring them back for more purchases.

It's important to keep in mind that the funnel doesn't work overnight. It does take time. Think about the first time you saw a Fashion Nova ad. You probably balked a little bit. Maybe you were even a little bit put off. That happened with a lot of people. When the first Fashion Nova ads went out, we were all very confused: "What is this? I will never buy that. I don't like this. This is probably

44

a scam." But over time, we saw more and more ads, and then we said, "Oh, these are clothes for curvy bodies. Oh, these are clothes for short girls. Oh, my God, they have a massive selection. And it's two-day shipping." We moved closer and closer to the point of conversion, and they got millions and millions of repeat shoppers. In a nutshell, that's what a funnel does, and now you know how to implement one.

CHAPTER 8

Turning Social Media into an Active Sales Channel

Many small business owners do not take social media seriously because they don't realize the value it brings. Social media is your key to hitting five-figure monthly sales basically for free, and many people don't want to believe that. Social media is the easiest, freest, cheapest, hardest-hitting way to get your product in front of people, keep them there, and get them into your store. My first six-figure sales month came from social media. My current businesses are fully supported by social media, organic and paid. That means organic posting as well as paid advertising. Social media is the lock and key to getting five, six, and seven figures a month in your business.

I want to make sure you really understand that social media is not a "nice to have," just as having a website for your business is now a non-negotiable. There was a point in time where, if you had a website, you were ahead of the curve. There was a point in time where, if you had social media, you were edgy. We're not there anymore. You need social media. It's now your best friend for marketing, and it needs to be built out correctly. It needs to be something you actively spend a lot of time on. Social media isn't an afterthought; it is a critical component of your marketing strategy.

Where most people go wrong is thinking they understand their customers when they really don't. Because it's social media, your personality is very likely to get unintentionally lumped into that, but you are not your shopper. You're not selling to yourself. You must understand who you're trying to get this content in front of and make sure your content communicates to them. The thing is, social media is very smart. Algorithms decide where to serve your content based on what it contains: what's in your script, what your hooks say, what your captions say, all of that. This all needs to be adjusted to get your content served to the people you're trying to reach.

For example, many BizTokers find themselves with no sales. They have 50k, 60k, 70k followers but no customers because they created content around building their business and got stuck in small-business TikTok. Who's buying there? Nobody. You need to stay out of BizTok and get in front of your customers. You do this by understanding who they are and making content that speaks to them.

Once you know who your target audience is, you need to understand what content you're going to post and how you're going to track its success. You're going to build out a system with different types of content. First, you're going to make content for a mass audience, pieces that anyone can consume and enjoy. They have a lot of reach, and the hope is that they become viral. You're going to follow that up with pieces that may get less reach but are more dialed into the people who have chosen to follow you after the previous mass exposure. You're going to have a broad mix of content that speaks to a mass audience but also communicates directly to your consumers.

For example, if you're selling sweaters, you might make a post about wearing your sweater to Target, something that's fun and anyone can enjoy. The follow-up to that would be posting something about the ethical standards of your business or maybe the comfiness and coziness of the sweater.

To take an example from real life, one of my previous clients sells a sweater with the world's biggest pockets. We did this really cute video where she stuffed the pockets full of everything you could imagine. She put in a shoe and then a pumpkin and then a hair-straightening iron, and then she had a really tiny dog that also went into the pocket. As you would expect, the content went viral. Everybody thought it was funny, and she got a big pump out of it. This piece of content didn't turn into tons of sales, but a lot of people had fun interactions with the brand. She followed it up with a piece about how her product is made, what it's made of, where it's made, and who makes it, and this turned into sales. That's how you want to play your own content.

When you're creating content, go quality over quantity, which is the dead opposite of what everyone else will tell you. Most people will say, "Make 10, 15, 20 pieces of content, post them all, and see which one sticks." I have a different opinion. I think you should spend more time on your hooks, your story, and making your content stand out. Send out three or four pieces, test them, and see what works. In this world of algorithms, the performance of one piece affects the performance of the next. If you send out 20 posts and none of them perform very well, the next post won't either. It's important to be intentional with what you're posting. Make sure it goes to the right place. Make sure it talks to your audience and keeps them hooked. That will help you build a healthy social media presence.

CHAPTER 9

Creating Compelling Content

Too many small-business owners fail to create compelling content. They think "creating" means putting something on the internet, and that equals content. They don't put the intentional work into crafting a piece their audience will enjoy. There's a really simple way to address this. It goes right back to understanding your target audience the same way you would when you're building your website and trying to source products: focus on things they care about—things they can relate to. As you're building your content strategy, it's important to write down how every single topic, every single concept, will make the customer feel. Then, mold your content around that.

For example, if you're selling slippers, don't just post a video with slippers in it because that does nothing for the viewer. No one's going to stop on the post because it's not interesting. It's not exciting. Instead, identify the most interesting and relevant aspect of this slipper that your audience will actually care about. Don't just say, "It's super cozy. It's super comfy. It's got a shearling fleece lining inside." These are all technical things that may not necessarily get someone to stop and scroll because we've all heard cozy, comfy, puffy, and sweet.

Instead, look at the features, process, or origin story of the slipper and present that to the viewer. Let's say our item is ethically made in LA and hand-sewn by a group of women. We're going to take one of those points and use that as our hook. It's much more compelling to say, "These slippers are handmade by women," than it is to say, "These slippers are so comfy and cozy." That's the difference that we're looking for when we're putting out content that needs to drive sales.

Let's start with the hook. Everything you think you know about hooks, I want you to forget. For a hook to be effective, it needs to be different from everyone else's. All those hooks the gurus tell you to use, like, "These seven things feel illegal to know about," or "I wish I had known this when I started my business," throw them out. Those hooks worked in the past, but at this point, they've been regurgitated by so many millions of people that they just aren't effective anymore. Never use a cookie-cutter hook. Every time you film, every time you draft, every time you whiteboard, think about the juiciest, most relevant aspect of the item you're presenting. Once you have that down, you have your hook down. Now, I want you to think of something called "triple hooking," using what people see, feel, and hear to draw them in.

Your first hook is going to be what comes out of your mouth, your audio. It's the first thing people hear, so it needs to be punchy—again, something like, "These slippers are handmade by a group of women," "Every one of these slippers is hand-sewn," or "These slippers are custom made in LA." Something dynamic and spicy. It can even be something off the wall, like, "I wore my slippers to Target today."

Now that you have your verbal hook, you're going to stack it with a visual hook—the first thing people see. For this to work, you want a nice background that catches people's attention and is slightly different from what they encounter in daily life. You're offering a "break," something people don't normally see. Most of the content people post doesn't get any views because it's "regular." They're showing you their living room, but you have your own living room. They're in their kitchen, but you have your own kitchen. Alternatively, if somebody's filming in their million-dollar kitchen, that's a scroll stopper.

With the visual hook, we're always looking for the most interesting area of the space we're in, and this is true no matter where you're shooting. If you're in your home and have a really nice corner of your house, with a big plant and really good lighting and just a tiny bit outside regular, that's what you want.

Let's say you live in a penthouse in LA and have this great city view. That's your visual hook. Or let's say you're walking around downtown and think there's nothing nearby that's particularly interesting. There are actually tons of things you can use, like public sculptures, a mirrored building that's glass all the way from top to bottom, or a really bushy tree. All of these are enough outside of regular that they help break up someone's feed and get them to stop.

Now we have two hooks: what we say and what people see. Our third hook adds another layer: text. It's critically important to spend time crafting this hook because so many people, more than 80 percent, watch TikTok, Reels, and YouTube with their audio off or very low. The text hook captures those people. This hook is similar to your verbal hook but worded a little differently. For example, if you say, "These slippers are custom made in LA," as your verbal hook, your on-screen text should be similar but different: "Custom-made Los Angeles slippers." This does two things: it gives you a good SEO score, which is really important, but it also traps people's eyeballs.

Now that you've covered what's spoken, seen, and read, you need to make sure your story is tight and compelling so people stay till the end. This is a little bit easier than writing your hook. All you need to do to pull this off is reduce words where you can, avoid duplication, and keep the pace fast so people don't get bored. Reset your frame every few seconds with a different shot, a different location. Then, wrap up with what I call the "offer." The offer can be very simple and is like a payoff. Shoppers will often have two questions when watching content: "Why am I still hanging around?"

and "What am I supposed to do now?" The offer answers those questions clearly and concisely.

Now that we've covered triple-hooking, I want to dial you in on why careful content creation is so relevant for your business. Many businesses these days are turning into six- and seven-figure businesses from social media alone. Not everybody learns how to create content the right way, but it's worth doing because it's one of the easiest ways to get viral exposure and reach for your brand, which will lead to more sales. In fact, all my businesses were built off social media alone and reached five figures a month before I even paid a dime on advertising.

Getting these core foundations for your content in place will give you a much better shot at building your business faster. This needs to be a priority, not an afterthought. Too many people treat content creation like they'll just get to when they get to. You need to prioritize it because it is your most valuable and brand-awareness place, and it's free. All you have to do is make a good piece of content and get it some views, and it will start generating sales.

Rather than spending time on ten other things and pushing off your social media until tomorrow, I want you to incorporate it into your active routine and spend an hour a day conceiving ideas, writing them down, filming, or editing, and make sure you get at least two to three pieces of content up on your business pages per week. Creating social media content for platforms like Instagram,

TikTok, YouTube Shorts, and Pinterest should not be something that you get to later; it's something you need to get to now.

The longer you wait to start growing on social media, the harder it's going to get. Remember the early days of Instagram, when it was pretty new, there weren't a lot of creators, and you would follow people more easily than you do now because there weren't a lot of accounts to follow, the platform wasn't saturated, and it was still fun? Other platforms like YouTube Shorts and TikTok are still in that space, and we also saw a little revival of that with Instagram Reels. The longer you wait and the older the platform gets, the harder it's going to be to get followers. Do it now. Now is the time.

Here are some key steps to creating effective videos, no matter the platform.

1. **You want to make them short and sweet**. The attention span for TikTok or Reels is about seven seconds. The amount of time you actually have to stop people and get them to pause on your video is about three seconds. You're not making a documentary; this is a quick hit.

2. **Brainstorming**. Brainstorming is really as simple as writing down ideas on a whiteboard and eliminating what isn't juicy. You might have ten ideas right now. Throw them up on the board, flesh them out, and cut out the ones that don't feel as exciting as the others. This will really help you boil your video down to what works and what doesn't.

3. **Make sure you have good lighting and sound**. Good lighting is one of the best ways to drive views on any social media platform because it makes content easier to process and enjoy. If you shoot a video in an area where everything is the same lighting, maybe the sun is at your back, and it's just not very enjoyable to watch, people will skip it. So, at the bare minimum, find good natural lighting or get a ring light. Audio is one of the easiest ways to ramp up views, and that doesn't mean trending audio videos of you dancing. It can be as simple as keeping your audio clean and pleasant. Don't have washers and dryers going off in the background. Don't film in echoey spaces. When you add audio to your videos, set it at a comfortable volume. You don't need to use a professional mic—simple $20 sets that plug into your phone can do the job. Keep in mind how your audio is going to make the viewer feel. Are you incorporating trending audio they can bounce along to and squeeze out a few extra seconds of watch time? Or is it your voice delivered in a clean, impactful way over a crispy mic? Because in the same way good audio can enhance the viewing experience, bad audio can be annoying and cause viewers to skip to end the misery of hearing loud, abrasive noises or music conflicting with your voice. Don't worry about being complicated. We're not talking god-level sound engineering. We just want something clean and pleasant.

CHAPTER 10

Getting More Traffic to Your Website

L et's discuss methods for getting traffic to your site—some well-known and others less so. Whether you already have some traffic or are just trying to get more, you can use both.

One of the lesser-known methods is to leverage niche communities or social media groups, joining them and sharing your business in a way that feels like you are sharing knowledge. For example, if you're a vintage seller, you can go to Reddit, find a forum on vintage stuff, and weigh in as a vintage expert. Link over to your business after demonstrating your authority, and that'll increase traffic. Will it increase by a thousand views a day? Probably not, but it will expose you to an audience that's very connected to what you're selling.

Another lesser-known method is to optimize for long-tail keywords. People are pretty familiar these days with SEO and keywords. Long-tail keywords are a little bit different; they are specific search terms that people use to look for things you might have. A regular keyword would be something like "cup" or "chair," but a long-tail keyword would be something like "luxury chairs for my dining room." Long-tail keywords ensure that when people google for specific items, they'll be directed to your site.

Then, we have guest blogging. This is a really obscure one. It's basically the same as finding niche communities. You are going to reach out to bloggers in your niche and offer to write guest posts for them. This will expose you to their audience and give you a new group of people who will see you as an authority figure backed by somebody they already know and love. This can do a lot for your traffic. It can take a little while, but it's well worth investigating and seeing if it's a good fit for your business.

One of the more well-known methods for drawing traffic is SEO. This is pretty simple. You're going to optimize your site for search engines using relevant keywords. You're also going to make relevant content, tag it appropriately, and build backlinks. SEO is important for making sure your site gets ranked properly. The key is to think beyond ranking for a single, simple item. For example, let's say you sell slippers. For slippers, ranking on the first page of Google—or the first three positions, which is really where the money is—is impossible. Somebody, probably some big corporation in your niche, already has those top spots. You're not going to get one unless you go in with billions of dollars. What you can do, though, is present your product as something more niche, focusing on something more specific about your brand that you can rank for. If your slippers are the puffiest, coziest slippers in the world, you can try to rank for the puffiest slippers. Ranking for something niche will literally skyrocket your traffic.

Another common method is social media marketing. This is usually the method everyone knows. While it's easy to know what it is, it can be hard to actually pull off. We talked a little bit about content creation earlier. You just need to make sure your social media game is ramped up.

Then, we have email marketing. Again, this is an old classic, something everybody does. You're going to have a list of subscribers, and you're going to regularly send out newsletters, but you're not just going to send, send, send because, if you have a high unopened rate, you're going to get penalized. Instead, you're going to test super-juicy subject lines and compelling titles to find what really motivates people to open their emails and click the links you've sent them.

CHAPTER 11

Photography

Using photography effectively is yet another critical point that can make or break your business, but people ignore it way too often. Photography is one of the first signals to a customer that they can trust you. It's not just nice to have; it is crucial to earning a sale. There are a few reasons for this. One, photography helps customers to visualize your product. It also shows that your business is legitimate. It builds trust because customers can see that you've made real efforts: you've spent money on a studio, and there's a real product here. It's not a slapped-together home business that's going to deliver subpar products or, worse, scam them.

When shoppers see high-quality photos that show off the item, they are much more likely to make a purchase. For example, with one of my previous businesses, I took a bunch of photos of my products. I knew they weren't movie quality, but I thought, "They get the job done." I took them with my iPhone and staged them nicely on a dining table with tissue paper and some glitter. I thought the photos were fine, and they worked well enough on Etsy. In reality, they were so bad that an ad agency I wanted to hire rejected me. They said nobody would buy my products based on those photos. This is the same agency that rejected me as a client because my website was so poor. Part of the reason for this was because my photos were terrible—and the ad agency knew they wouldn't turn into sales. I spent a few hundred dollars and a month reshooting all my products, and sure enough, it made a huge difference in sales.

That's how important good photography is. Good photos build trust, show people that you're real, and give you a level of authenticity. They show shoppers that you take your business seriously, so they're going to take it seriously. Good photos increase conversions for a lot of different reasons, but the simple fact is the better your photos are, the more customers understand what they're buying.

Photography can also be used to differentiate your brand. There are no rules that say you have to have a white background in photos of your product. You can do whatever you want. You just need to make sure it's cohesive, and your photos are consistent. What you don't want to do is shoot ten different products on ten different backdrops with ten different lighting styles. It will feel disjointed. What would work instead would be to shoot ten different products in ten different shades of the same color. The goal here is consistency.

Strong product photos can set you apart and make your brand storytelling shine through in an impactful way, but they have to be cohesive. Everything needs to look and feel the same. The background, lighting, editing, and crop ratios all need to be the same for every item. Now, I'm not saying your hero image needs to be the same proportions or have the same crop ratio and lighting as your product listing photos, but all of your product listing photos do need to have the same theme.

The next type of photo you need is of the product being used. It's crucial that shoppers visualize the product in their lives, and one of the best ways to do that is to show somebody actually using it. If you're selling hair scrunchies, you're going to want a shot of somebody with a scrunchie in their hair. Not only that, but you're going to want to show different ways they can be used. Scrunchies can be worn on the wrist. They can be tied around a bag in a cute little knot. They can sit on your dresser next to all your jewelry. Super cute. Shoppers do not get to physically see the product until they have already purchased it, so we have to recreate the shopping experience for them through photos. This means they need to be able to see, smell, touch, feel, and envision this thing in their hand. We do that with an effective combination of photos.

This next bit of advice is a really big one. If you listen to nothing else that I've said in this entire chapter, listen to this: make sure your product photos are focused on the product. Too many people try too hard to stylize the photo, making it difficult to know what's for sale. The product gets completely lost. If you're selling a candle, you don't want to set it on a dining table with a turkey, a few other candles, a bunch of cups, forks, knives, and a tablecloth because shoppers will have no idea what's for sale. You do want styling, but you don't want it to obscure or even overshadow the product.

In the same vein, the hero image on your website needs to be a very tight shot of the product or your collections. For example, let's say you're selling perfume. A simple picture of a perfume bottle staged on a gold shelf, with a few accessories next to it but the focus on the bottle, would work. If you sell rings, a close-up of a model's hands close to her face would work. What wouldn't work is a photo of a big pile of jewelry if you're trying to get people to understand which items are yours. If you sell sweaters, you don't want your hero image to be a bunch of blankets thrown over a couch. The idea is that the image needs to be tightly focused on the product so there is no mistaking what is being sold. Otherwise, people won't understand what's for sale—or even worse, they'll think you're selling one of the other items in the photo.

Finally, you want to use extremely high-quality pictures, the best you can get, with the best lighting and focus, anything to make your photos look professional. If you need to hire a professional photographer to do this, do it. It will pay for itself. You also want to make sure you get shots of the product from different angles. Doing so shows off the products' textures and details from top to bottom so shoppers can get a good grasp of what they're buying.

Product photography can make all the difference in your business. Good photos convert, while bad photos throw people off your brand and make them not trust you. Keep everything cohesive, maintain the same crop ratios and branding, and keep the focus on the product itself.

CHAPTER 12

Creating High-Conversion Listings

High-conversion listings require a delicate balance of storytelling and information. The dos and don'ts are actually pretty simple. Number one, incorporate storytelling into the first part of your listing. This creates an emotional connection with the shopper. It can be the story behind your brand, the origins of the product itself, scent notes if you're selling a perfume or a candle, or what inspired the product. Mainly, though, it's going to tell the customer how the product will make their life better. If you're selling something cozy, this is the place to do it. You're going to create an emotional bridge here with the customer. It's very important to do this, and a lot of people miss it.

The next piece of our listing is the technical specs. These need to be strategically placed because, if we tell a good story, customers will want to find them to make sure the product will actually fit into their lives the way they want it to. There are a few ways to do this. One is to put the specs directly after your storytelling. Another option, if you're a little more advanced with coding or have a website developer, is to put them on a separate tab. This is really popular and converts well, as it keeps things nice and separated. The specs should include things like measurements in inches, size charts, and product capabilities. Anything that's too sterile for the storytelling part but is critically important goes in your tech spec section.

Next comes the images. We have talked a lot about images, but they are absolutely critical to pushing people into conversions. All those great shots of products you took are going into your listings. You want to aim for between five and 10, depending on what niche you're in. If you're selling something like tech, you probably only need four or five. If you're selling clothing, you're going to want to have more rather than less because clothing is one of those things where people really want to make sure it fits. A combination of product, lifestyle, and styled shots will make it easy for shoppers to understand and feel why they should buy the product.

When crafting your listings, you need to use very simple language. The text needs to be clear as day, super tight, concise, and easy to understand. This is not the place for technical jargon. Keep that for your technical specs. The reason for this is that as people move through your site, they're scanning and skimming. Nobody wants to do a deep dive on products until they're in that headspace. Your listings need to be as clear, short, sweet, simple, and impactful as possible. I have a little recipe for how to do this. We're going to start with the title, which is the first thing shoppers usually see.

Often, shoppers look at the title before the image, so it's important to make it as punchy as possible. Use words that paint a picture of the product and how it's going to benefit the shopper. You want to keep the title between 50 and 80 characters so it's simple to read and doesn't get cut off in search results. And use keywords. When people use Google or the search function on your site, they're going to look for keywords, so be sure to have a few sprinkled into your titles.

Here's an example of what not to do with your titles. Let's say you're selling a cashmere sweater. If your title is something like "Cashmere Sweater," that's not very exciting to a shopper. What might be more exciting is "Luxe Cashmere Holiday Sweater." The idea is to be as punchy as you can and give as much information as you can, but do it in as few words as possible. You also need to make sure your titles differentiate your products from each other. If you sell nothing but sweaters but have ten sweaters called "Cozy Cashmere Sweater," that's not going to help. Use different identifiers in your titles, or even name your products. This will help with Google ranking and searchability.

Next, we're going to write a compelling description. The chances of people buying from you go up a lot when they see how your product can solve their problems or fulfill their desires. Believe it or not, fulfilling someone's desire is solving a problem. A shopper's problem can really be as simple as "I feel cold and want something warm" or "I want to feel good, so I want to buy something." Focus on benefits rather than rattling off the product's features. Focus on how it's going to improve their quality of life. Instead of saying something like, "Our handmade leather bag will last a lifetime and age beautifully," go with something more along the lines of, "Our handcrafted leather bags, created with premium materials, will last a lifetime and age beautifully." The description needs to trigger emotions in the shopper, and it does so through sensory language.

Sensory language helps people to imagine what it's like to own your product. It puts the product in their hands. For example, if you're selling a candle, you can say something along the lines of, "The crisp scent of our handmade candles will transport you to a cozy winter evening by the fireplace." It's simple—and a little bit corny—but it also transforms your shopper's headspace, bringing them to a warm fireplace with a nice scented candle.

Lastly, you're going to create a sense of urgency. Most importantly, you're going to use CTA, telling the customer, "Shop now." You can also use low-stock timers and limited-time offers to increase the urgency. For example, you can say the product is "in 10 other people's carts." There are a lot of ways to do this. Sometimes, it can be as simple as "Add to Cart." Tell them where to go. Tell them what to do.

CHAPTER 13

Pricing Products for Profit

F ew things are more important to your business's success than getting the pricing right, whether you're just starting out or thinking about changing your prices. Starting too low puts you at a disadvantage and risks losing money unnecessarily. Pricing too high can prevent shoppers from buying.

Now, many of you might say this is obvious advice, but before you brush past this chapter, keep in mind: where you price is almost always where you stay. For example, if you start your business with a low-cost pricing strategy but then want to raise prices later on, that's going to be tough because shoppers will associate you with bargains. For example, Walmart would never be able to sell luxury goods—their customers don't go there for that. On the other hand, if you're trying to sell luxury items but come in priced too low, shoppers won't take you seriously as a luxury establishment. Pricing is hard—and it should be because it's incredibly important. If you're finding that pricing is "easy," you're probably doing it wrong, and it's worth taking a step back to make sure your product is priced in a way that maximizes sales.

A classic trap too many business owners fall into is underpricing by underestimating costs. For example, if you're selling a $15 dress with $5 shipping and running Meta Ads, you're going to be in the negative real quick. Why? Because the cost of acquiring a paying customer through ads can be anywhere from $12 to $45 on average. Think about that. You'd be selling at a loss. You'd be paying to sell. Just because you "can" sell something for $15 doesn't mean that's the right price for profit.

Part 1: Getting Started with Pricing

- **Figuring Out Your Costs**: First things first, work out how much it costs you to make your product. This includes everything from materials to labor. Knowing this helps you set a price that covers your costs and earns you a profit.

- **Checking Out the Competition**: Take a look at what others are charging for similar stuff. This gives you a ballpark figure for what customers are willing to pay and helps you find a sweet spot for your own prices.

- **Your Product's Special Sauce**: Think about what makes your product special or different from others. If it offers something unique, you might be able to charge a bit more.

Part 2: Why Pricing Right Is Key for Profit

- **Avoiding Pricing Pitfalls**: If your price is too low, you might not make enough profit. The price is too high, and customers might go elsewhere. It's all about finding a balance.

- **Tweaking Prices Over Time**: Markets change, costs change, and so should your prices. Keep an eye on things and adjust your prices when needed to stay profitable. This doesn't mean drastic price increases or decreases; it means making moderate changes as the market shifts.

- **Price Equals Perception**: Remember, people often link price to quality. Too cheap might look low-quality, while a higher price can give off a high-quality vibe.

Part 3: Fine-Tuning Your Prices

- **Watching Your Sales**: If stuff isn't flying off the shelves, your prices might be too high. But if you're selling out fast, maybe your prices are too low, and you could make more profit.

- **Profit Check-Up**: Make sure your prices are high enough to cover costs and leave you with a good profit. If not, it might be time for a price hike.

- **Listening to Customers**: What do your customers think about your prices? Their feedback can help you figure out if you need to make adjustments.

- **Conclusion:** Setting the right price for your products is critical for your business's success. Keep these points in mind to create a pricing strategy that works for you and keeps your business profitable.

CHAPTER 14

Using Customer Service to Drive Sales

Exceptional customer service is one of the best customer retention tactics because it gives people something to come back for—it makes them feel valued. Think about the early days of Amazon, when you could return anything you wanted, no questions asked. You felt safe buying from them because you knew the customer service was there. You felt assured you were going to be totally secure in your Amazon purchase. That was an intentional move on Amazon's part, and it actually kept them from being profitable for several years. Their goal was to be the pinnacle of trustworthiness through customer service because they knew it would pay off in the long run. It paid off for them in the biggest way possible, turning them into the biggest platform with the most reach and the most customers. That's how big of a deal customer service is in creating strong fan bases, repeat customers and overall shopper loyalty.

Outstanding customer service helps you build strong relationships with your customers and makes them want to come back for more. It also has the positive side effect of getting people to recommend your business to friends and family for free. In a nutshell, great customer service turns into free marketing for you. You went above and beyond to make sure your customers were happy, so they are now more than happy to tell other people about your brand and how it prioritizes caring for their shoppers.

Now, probably the least known effect of good customer service is that it can give you a competitive advantage because too many people treat it as a byproduct of doing business, something that has to happen to keep the machine running. Good customer service is the bare minimum, but exceptional customer service can differentiate your brand. Offering superior service to your shoppers is a solid way to separate yourself from other players in the market, and it can do a lot for your brand growth.

One of the best practices for exceptional customer service is listening actively. When a customer reaches out with a question or a concern, it's easy to see it as one of many. Keep in mind that this is a real person with a real problem, and listen very carefully to what they have to say. You need to craft an empathetic response. Try to understand their situation and take the time to find out what it is they want to see resolved.

Next, you're going to respond quickly. Customers value fast responses. Whether they're asking for a return, have a question about a product, or are looking for coupons, no matter what it is, the faster you can respond, the happier the customer will be, and the better chance you have of turning them into a sale.

You also need to go above and beyond. This means looking for any opportunities to blow customers away. This doesn't mean giving discounts. It means offering a personalized recommendation. When a customer has a question about a product, it means saying, "Hey, you might like this." If they ask, "Will this match with this?" or "What sizes will this come in?" providing them personal answers, additional resources, or even following up just to make sure that they are happy will make them see you differently than your competition.

This next suggestion is going to seem a little odd. You're going to use positive language when talking to your customers. Always use friendly language and avoid negative or confrontational words. This subtly reinforces positive thoughts in the shopper and improves their perception of your business.

Probably the biggest suggestion of all of these is to train your team. Everyone needs to be on the same page about what the standard of customer service is. So, whether you work with a friend, family member, or husband, or maybe you have a full team, everybody must know the protocol when it comes to customer service. All inquiries and issues are handled with the same level of positive, personalized, exceptional customer service to set your business apart.

When you implement these suggestions, you will be seen as somebody with exceptional customer service, and that's how you differentiate yourself in a really crowded market. The more satisfied and valued you can get your customers to feel, the happier they're going to be and the more likely they'll choose your product or service over a competitor's.

CHAPTER 15

Building Your Email and SMS List

Most people understand how building your email list works, but they're not great at doing it. Let's talk about how to do it the right way, and we're going to break it down into a few parts. Start with building your email list effectively. This is going to look a lot different than just having a pop-up or an opt-in on your website that says, "Put in your email." It's going to be a lead magnet.

One of the best ways to build your email list is to create a compelling offer that gives value to a potential customer. A lead magnet for an e-commerce store could be something like a discount code or free shipping, something you're already probably familiar with. But it could also be a free download, a free eBook, a PDF, or something that educates people about your products. It could also be a quiz or a survey.

Quizzes are really fun, and they're a cool way to get people involved in your products without asking them for anything. It feels like you're actually giving them something. You've probably seen these before on websites selling skincare or haircare. You take a short quiz, and then, at the end, you receive a coupon code to buy this thing that the website has recommended is good for you. It feels personalized; you gamified the whole experience.

What won't work as a lead magnet is having a pop-up that says, "Give me your email." Another example is a pop-up that says, "Give me your email, and I'll give you 5% off." It's sterile and dry, but not only that, the offer is too low for anyone to care about, which is why a lot of the big brands will offer 15% off, 20% off, etc. The offer needs to be good enough that, as a shopper, I am willing to trade my information for it.

Another effective way to grow your list is through exit-intent pop-ups, which appear when people leave your site. Used too frequently or aggressively, they can annoy people, but they can be very effective when used strategically. You're going to follow the same recipe of using language that fits your brand tone. As shoppers exit the website, they'll receive an offer to join your email list. Ideally, it should be a little bit better than the first offer they encountered. Maybe they entered the website and skipped an offer for 10% off if they joined the email list, but you really don't want to lose them. Create an exit-intent pop-up with an offer of 15% off. It's a great way to capture people who otherwise might just leave your site.

Social media contests can be used to grow your list as well. They give people the opportunity to get something for free, an actual, tangible product, and all they have to do is sign up. Now, a word of caution with these. Even though they can help you grow your list and expand your reach, many people who opt-in will not be as qualified as your regular customers. There will be a lot of looky-loos who just want to get in on something free, and many will never intend to purchase. That's one of the hazards of running a social media contest, but if executed properly and handled with the right expectations, they can be worthwhile.

Part two is building your SMS list, or texting list. SMS lists are converting really well these days. The open rate on them is really high. They feel more personal. People are much more likely to look at a brand's text than an email. So, if you can build your SMS list, it's a great way to pull people back to your website.

Much the same way you would use an email list, you will use the SMS list to offer exclusive discounts and updates on product drops. You're going to optimize the process, making it easy for people to opt into the list and explaining the benefits of why they should—but you need to make absolutely clear that they are doing so. To help with this, you can use a double opt-in process to confirm their subscription. This also reduces the risk of spam complaints.

Now that we have a plan for collecting email addresses and phone numbers, let's talk about crafting emails and texts to our subscribers and turning them into superfans because that's really what we're trying to do. The technique we are going to use is something called the "Welcome Aboard" or "Welcome Series." A lot of people miss out on this opportunity, but they are great for building relationships with customers. Your Welcome Aboard series should be structured as several emails that follow one another. The first one is a gratitude email, a simple "Thank you for joining." An example I like to use for this is a plant store. The first email they're going to send would say something like, "Thank you for joining our green family. We can't wait to help you grow your indoor jungle." The message is aligned with the brand's tone, but it's fun, and importantly, it's not asking for anything. It's thanking the customer and welcoming them.

After the gratitude email, we're going to send an introduction email. The introduction is going to talk about who you are as a business. Continuing with the plant store, they might start the email with something like, "We started our journey five years ago. Our vision was to bring nature indoors." Then, they would talk a little about the plants and the store's core message: "Our plants are carefully grown and hand-picked for their beauty and easy care." Again, they're not asking for anything; they're just warming people up.

Next, we send a preview email. This email is very important for establishing what people can expect from your sequences. Done right, it can decrease the risk of people unsubscribing or getting annoyed at getting so many emails. Very simply, the email says something like, "You can expect biweekly emails" or "You can expect an update once a month." A good example of this from the plant store would be: "You can expect emails twice a week with plant care tips, new arrivals, and exclusive deals." So, they're giving plant tips for free, but they're also keeping the emails loaded with value.

The fourth email sent out is the incentive email. This is where you start offering discounts. This could be something like, "Here's $20 off your first plant baby as a welcome to our family." With this last email, you've mapped out an entire introductory welcome series that makes people feel included, and you didn't ask for anything until the end.

Let's dig into subject lines and hooks. Just as our website content needs a hook, our emails do, too. The better your email hook is, the greater the chance somebody will actually open it and read it. For example, let's say you have a coffee company, and your email goes out under the title "Your Morning Brew." Or maybe it says, "Brewing Guide: Getting the Most from Your Beans," and the email includes three new roasts for your customers. The title suggests there's something of value in the email and makes the customer want to open it.

Convincing customers to open your emails is critical to preventing them from being blocked by a spam filter. If your email goes out with a high unopened rate, you're going to get penalized. To avoid such filters, you need to be very careful about what they like and don't like. If you sell fitness clothes, you might see better open rates if you change your subject line from "The Biggest Sale Ever," which a spam filter is not going to like, to "Get Fit For Less."

Next, let's talk about finding your frequency. This is huge for establishing consistency with your customers. The right frequency will not only increase your open rate but will get people to understand when they should expect something from you. If you have a bakery, you might find it's more effective to reduce your emails to twice a week. Instead of sending email after email focused on getting people in the door, maybe on Tuesdays, you send recipes, and on Fridays, you send special menu items. Finding your frequency will help prevent shoppers from becoming fatigued by your emails, but it also gives them something to look forward to, especially if you're offering something of value.

Lastly, let's look at emails that convert into sales. Personalization is critical for sales emails. If you're going to send a dry email without calling out the shopper by name, they're going to feel a little bit jaded because most people are accustomed to being addressed by their name in emails, especially when they sign up for an email list.

Another way to tailor your emails is to send customized recommendations to shoppers based on products they've previously bought. You can track this with software on the backend. If "Christina" bought a night cream, send emails that say, "Hi, Christina. Your night cream pairs well with…" followed by a product recommendation that complements the purchase already made. Such an email shows that you care about your customer and their purchase and that you are here to help and give them the best experience with your brand. Putting a button or link at the end of the email that says something like, "Complete your skincare routine," will make it easy for them to add that additional purchase to their cart. You've personalized the email, made sure it felt special to them, and then told them, "Here's where you go to buy it."

CHAPTER 16

Identifying Key Marketing Channels

Finding the right marketing channel for any business is a key point of success because your shoppers live in different places. If you market to them in the wrong area, not only are you not going to find them, but you're going to waste a ton of money. By finding and marketing on the most effective channels, you can maximize your ad spend and get the best return on your investment.

On the other hand, if you choose the wrong channels, you end up wasting not just time but resources on marketing efforts that produce no results. That happens because your audience isn't there. You're just sending your products and money out into the void. The obvious channels, like Facebook, Instagram, and X (formerly Twitter), are great for small businesses, but not every business has the same results on all social media platforms. If you are targeting an older audience, you might find that your audience lives on Facebook, so if you try to set up your ads on something like TikTok, you're probably just going to spend a lot of money and not get anything back. But if your audience tends to be very political or tech-savvy, you might find that they're on LinkedIn or X. In that case, you want to focus your efforts there.

People often think, *I'll use Facebook, Instagram, and X,* and they put the same amount of money and creativity on all the different platforms. They end up wasting most of their money on their ad spend because their audience doesn't live on half the platforms they chose. This can also be said for Google placements. Some people have really good results on Google because their audience is the type that uses the search engine to find what they want. Some people have better results just by going the social media route. It's not enough to know who your audience is; you also need to know where they live—and where they "live" is where they spend their digital time. Find out where they're spending their time online and attack their feed there.

Email marketing takes a lot of maintenance, but it has the benefit of reaching people who are already pretty interested in what you want to sell. If you're sending out a weekly or monthly email, it should be customized and tailored to the shopper. It's great if you can add details like, "You were considering this" or "You might also like this." One thing you should realize about email marketing: *it doesn't tend to produce a lot of results right away.* It's an overtime kind of thing, very important for your overall strategy, but it doesn't work in the same way as other types of marketing.

We also have SEO, which a lot of people don't realize is marketing. SEO essentially just means optimizing your website to rank higher. It means crawling your way to the top of Google searches, and this is critically important because, on Google, the top three shops get the lion's share of traffic, with number one getting the most. Whoever has that top spot on Google when you search is getting almost all of the people. Number two is getting the next, and number three is getting most of what's left. Anything below that is getting essentially nothing, so it's kind of not even worth it to have a ranking on Google unless you can get to the top three.

The competitiveness of Google means you need a strong SEO strategy. As I mentioned earlier in this book, companies spend billions of dollars trying to get the top rank. Unless you have the same, the most effective way to use Google is to find something you can rank in. You aren't going to rank under something like clothing. The top spots are taken by Target, Fashion Nova, or some of the other big guys. But you can rank in things that are more specific to your store, things that are specialties. So, maybe you sell cute winter clothes for adventurous people. Rather than trying to go for the biggest thing you could rank for, go for the niche things and try to get a higher rank there.

Next, we have influencer marketing. Everyone knows what this is. You partner with social media influencers who are interested in your product. One thing I want to say about this is that they do not have to be mega-influencers. You do not need to work with people who have 250,000 followers or a million followers.

You want to approach this by trying to get the most bang for your buck, and a lot of times, that means micro-influencers. Micro-influencers tend to have 10,000 followers or fewer; usually, between 1,000 and 10,000 will put you in that micro-influencer space. They have a higher reach with their audience because smaller accounts get served to more of their followers. The larger an account grows, the less reach it gets. That's just the way the algorithms work.

One of the big upsides with micro-influencers is that they have greater reach to their audience. They're more engaged. They're more plugged in. At this point, they're still a real person with their followers, so they're still very connected. They spend time in their comment section, and they respond to people.

On top of that, they're often better with things like deadlines and production quality because they're still trying to impress brands and get more deals. They're also a lot cheaper. For all these reasons, I choose to work almost exclusively with micro-influencers. One of the added benefits is that micro-influencers will often give you bundles.

Something to consider here: a mega-influencer may want $4,000 for one post, while a micro-influencer might give you three posts for $500. This is extremely valuable because then you're hitting multiple touchpoints with their audience. Let's say you have $4,000 to spend on your influencer marketing this quarter. It would be a better use of your money to take ten micro-influencers, get a few posts from each, and spread that $4,000 among them. You get more reach, more engagement, and multiple exposures to a niche audience that's interested in your products versus a one-off, one-time post with a mega-influencer.

That being said, mega-influencers are good for one thing that is crucial to growing a business, and that is social proof. In some cases, if your revenue supports it, it might make sense to take that $4,000 and give it to a huge influencer with a million followers just to say that that influencer wore your product, and now you have the social proof. It's not going to be a big revenue driver immediately, but you will now be able to say, "As seen on," and social proof turns into money. Depending on where you're at with your business, you need to think hard about which strategy best matches your goals when you're approaching influencer marketing.

Let's get into actually identifying the right markets for your small business. Understanding your target audience—and I know you're sick of hearing this—is vital because, if you don't, you won't know where they're most likely to engage with your brand. We determine that with channel mapping.

Channel mapping is going through the marketing landscape and figuring out where you're going to place your marketing. For example, you have a small bakery that specializes in organic, gluten-free products, and your marketing channels right now are social media, and you're looking at local markets. You're going to create a list of the marketing channels you plan to explore, and then you're going to research their potential reach and engagement among your target audience. Then, we're going to move to channel prioritization. This means choosing where to focus.

Let's say you evaluate the potential reach of each marketing channel and discover that social media appears to have the biggest potential for growth of your target audience. It seems to be where people are the most active. You figure out that people love to share pictures of baked goods, and they like to have a little "experience" or "ritual" when they visit a bakery. Based on that, you think social media is going to be the most viable marketing option because you can create port-worthy goods for your shoppers. But you also know that foot traffic is going to come from your local community. Social media is valuable for getting a lot of attention, but you still need to be plugged in with your local community to actually get people through the door and pay the bills.

Now, you can prioritize based on this information and choose which channel you're going to put the most effort into first. Armed with this data, you can start using social media marketing and participate in local events and partnerships, maybe even collaborate with other coffee shops or bakeries, people in your niche with complimentary products that don't compete with yours. In this way, you can expand your reach to their audience without competing. Assess the potential of each of the marketing channels on the list we created and prioritize them based on the relevance to your business first, your target audience next, and then available resources to find the best ROI. After you've done this, it's time to do some channel comparisons.

Comparing channels boils down to weighing their pros and cons. What are the pros of social media marketing, and what are the cons? What are the pros of local marketing, and what are the cons? Pros for social media are pretty easy. It's basically free and has a high chance of going viral if you know what you're doing. As for cons, it's very, very time-consuming, requires consistent content creation, and means engaging with people 24-7, being friendly, and always being on. Local marketing, on the other hand, is not free. You have to pay an entry fee, you have to buy a tent, and you have to show up and bring your products in person. But the time commitment is a lot less.

Let's say you've finished weighing the pros and cons of your marketing channels and decided it's viable to do both. Now, you're going to look into channel fit. This means aligning channels with your brand. You do this by ensuring consistency in all the areas you've decided fit with your brand identity.

By now, you've developed a brand identity, created guidelines across your marketing channels, and made everything consistent so it feels, looks, smells, and tastes the same online and in the bakery. Now that you have a pretty robust understanding of your marketing channels, we're going to move into channel diversification, maximizing reach and mitigating risks.

By focusing on your social media and email marketing, you'll recognize the importance of diversifying your marketing efforts. Maybe they're not producing the volume you wanted, maybe growth is a little slower than you expected, or maybe you even recall that time back in 2020 when we lost Instagram for a day, and everyone thought we were going to be knocked offline. This is why you diversify. Maybe you'll collaborate with local influencers and bloggers to expand your reach through their networks. This can also mean partnering with complementary businesses and cross-promoting each other's products. To continue our bakery example, if the coffee store across the street offers ground coffee, you can exchange products to showcase in each other's stores. You're not competing; you're complementing one another, and you both get to double your reach.

I want you to identify additional marketing channels that may not seem obvious but align with your business goals and target audience. Research your competitors. See what channels they're using and how successful they are at it. This is pretty easy to do, especially if you use something like the Meta Ad Library. You can see what ads people are running and how effective they are.

After you gather this information, you're going to start looking for gaps in the market that your business can fill. If you run a bakery, search for areas that other bakeries haven't tapped into. See how you can fill those gaps in the market. Your bakery might already be selling gluten-free products, but what about designer cupcakes?

That's a product with mass demand that not a lot of small bakeries can accommodate. Maybe no one in your area is doing that yet. That's what you're looking for—unfilled opportunities.

CHAPTER 17

Analyzing and Optimizing Your Marketing Strategy

I t's time to analyze the systems we put in place for marketing and evaluate how efficient they actually are. To do this, you must first define objectives. You can't skip this step. Get real about what you're trying to accomplish. Are you aiming to increase your brand awareness, or are you trying to get people to your website? Maybe you want more leads. Whatever it is, you need to be clear about it because if you don't have an objective, you have nothing to measure, and you're going to end up with scrambled results.

Once you know what your goals are, you can begin to understand if your marketing efforts have been effective. First, you need to understand KPIs—key performance indicators. KPIs are measurable values that show how effective your marketing strategy is at achieving your objectives. They tell you in clear, simple terms if your actions are paying off. KPIs vary based on what you're trying to do. For example, if you're trying to drive traffic to your website, your KPI might be the number of clicks on links to your website. Another would be your CTR—click-through rate.

Essentially, the CTR tells you how many people clicked on a link or an ad compared to how many people saw it. It's like a gauge of how effective your online content is at getting people to take action. The higher the CTR, the more successful your content engages users and prompts them to click through to your website or landing page. It tells you how many people go from looking at something to clicking through to the other side. To get this number, you're going to divide the number of link clicks by the number of impressions. Often, you don't have to do this. Most software has this function built in, but it's important to know what your click-through rate is because if you're below a certain value, there's something wrong.

You need to be an expert in your industry. I want you to look up your industry, find out what a healthy click-through rate is for your specific niche, and then tweak your site until you hit that number. If you're above it, great. If you're right at it, that's great, too. But if you're significantly below it, then you need to work on some things.

Another KPI you can measure is your bounce rate. This is the percentage of visitors who leave the site after looking at only one page. For example, people who land on your hero image have a quick look, maybe take half a scroll, and then boom, they leave. The bounce rate measures the number of people who get to your site but then leave before doing anything. You really want to know your bounce rate because if shoppers are hitting your website, it means they're interested enough to click through. But if you're using paid ads to get them there, only for them to bounce off, you're spending money just for them to look at your site and then leave. If the bounce rate is really, really high, it means there's something wrong with the page they're landing on, and you need to adjust it.

Next, we have channel-specific analytics. Most platforms these days have tools that give you specific performance data. This includes Meta, Instagram, X Analytics, and Google Analytics. You're going to want to get familiar with all of these, but you're also going to take it further and look at your analytics for things like Klaviyo or Mailchimp (online platforms designed for e-commerce marketing and email automation). Analyze the reach and engagement of all your content. If you have high reach but low engagement, that means a lot of people are seeing your content. This might seem great, but very few people are interacting with it, meaning the site is not compelling them to move forward. This could be for a number of reasons: the images are not strong enough, the copy is poor, or maybe what you're saying in the ads isn't working. In general, if you have high reach and a lot of impressions but low engagement, it means that even though people are seeing your site, they're not interested enough to interact with it.

Similarly, posts or emails that are meant to drive traffic to your website should have a high number of link clicks. If they don't, you need to readjust your CTA or the content itself. Usually, it is the content that needs work.

I learned from a marketing mentor that "Nine times out of ten, if an ad isn't working, the creative is bad." This means that a lot of people think that all you have to do for an ad is set up an image, throw up some text, and make sure it's targeting. They spend all their effort on making sure the targeting is correct without actually making creative that pulls people in. Creative is what people see. The old saying, "People eat with their eyes," means they consume with their eyeballs; that's how you talk to their soul. So, just as important as targeting the right people with the ad is making sure that what they're seeing in the ad is appealing and makes them want to click through it.

CTAs are the next thing to analyze. They are not as important as your creative, but they're still important. For example, if you're selling shoes and your CTA says, "Learn More," that might be mismatched with the ad and not driving as many clicks as "Shop Now" would. On the other hand, if you're selling a service and you mistakenly use "Shop Now" as your CTA rather than "Learn More," it would feel disjointed. Make sure that your CTA aligns with your creative, your targeting, and the overall flow of your ad.

Based on what you collect within these analytical areas, you're going to make adjustments. If your marketing is not giving you the results you want, or if it's giving you no results at all, it's time to adjust. This means you need to start experimenting with different types of content to see what's pulling in the audience the most. Which ones are resonating with shoppers?

I've seen this play out multiple times. One of my main businesses is Puffie Slippers, which started as a struggling brand with virtually no sales. I tried everything in my ads: listing photos, model shots, and graphics. One day, out of pure frustration, I decided I was just going to make a silly little ad in Canva. I didn't even think about it. I was mad. I slapped together a bright gradient background, dropped each pair of slippers into a cute little arch, added some graphics, labeled it "Astro Puffies" at the top, and put a "Shop Now" icon at the bottom. The ad went bananas despite the fact that it was the same product, the same ad spend, and the same targeting. Everything else had brought in pale results, but this ad started bringing in hundreds and hundreds of dollars a day.

So many times, it just comes down to the right creative, but you're not going to find the right creative until you start testing. The more you know your audience, the better you will be at creating effective tests. You also need to test different CTAs. Find out which ones best motivate your audience to take the desired action. Whether it's "Shop," "Shop Now," "Visit Site," or "Add to Cart," you're going to figure out which ones shoppers like the most, which ones pull in the highest click-through rate, which ones result in the most purchases, and you're going to keep adjusting the CTAs over time because these things change. What works today may not work next month. So, when things start to dip or slow down, it's time to test some more.

Conclusion and Next Steps

Congratulations on finishing the 5-Figure Formula! Seriously, not everyone sticks it out to the end of a book, especially one about building an e-commerce business. Most people quit before they even start, so you're already ahead of the curve.

I wrote this book to help people improve their lives, business, and financial future, and I hope it's given you the confidence to chase freedom for you and your loved ones. Now, take what you've learned and put it to work in your business.

If you're an aspiring entrepreneur, just start! Today. Don't overthink it. There's nothing like building a business that makes a difference using your mind, body, and soul. If you're a seasoned pro, you're probably thinking about your next move. The journey never stops, so take it one step at a time and celebrate the small wins.

Whether you're just starting out or a veteran, you can either figure it out through trial and error like I did, or you can work with me and my team to speed up the process by months, maybe even years.

If you want some help building and scaling your brand, check out my private community for e-commerce business owners, the Six-Figure Growth Community. Right now, I do a live masterclass every month for serious business owners, but that might change soon.

Since you bought this book, I want to give you a discount so you can join my community and work directly with me. If you've read this entire book, I know you're serious about your business!

Head to **www.sixfiguregrowth.community** to sign up for my next masterclass.

I get super excited by sharing how I've grown multiple brands to five figures a month and helped others hit six figures. No one can guarantee results, but being around people chasing the same goals definitely ups your chances.

If you want personal guidance and support on your journey, I'd be honored to help you both professionally and personally.

Whatever comes next, I hope our paths cross again. Wishing you all the best!

THANK YOU FOR READING MY BOOK!

Thank you for reading my book!

Here are a few free bonus resources.

Scan the QR Code Here:

I appreciate your interest in my book and value your feedback as it helps me improve future versions of this book. I would appreciate it if you could leave your invaluable review on Amazon.com with your feedback. Thank you!

www.ingramcontent.com/pod-product-compliance
Lightning Source LLC
LaVergne TN
LVHW042339060326
832902LV00006B/268